Principles of Microeconomics Explained

Can Akdeniz

First Publishing, 2015

ISBN-10: 1519745346
ISBN-13: 978-1519745347

Baderstrasse 55
D-53489 Bad Bodendorf
Germany

Web: http://www.businesshacker.co

Contents

Book Description

Whether you are an economics student, or a businessman, or you run a shop, or you manage a restaurant, this course is essential for you on the grounds that it helps you in different economic situations.

This helpful course is about *Principles of Microeconomics*. You must read this course to clear your concepts regarding Microeconomics.

What you'll learn in this book:

- The Basics of Economics
- Introduction to Microeconomics
- Economic Growth
- Demand and Supply
- Markets, Maximizers, and Efficiency
- Productivity and Equity
- Public Goods
- Production and Costs
- Competitive Markets for Goods and Services
- Lots, lots more!

Make your decision now, without wasting your time anymore, buy it now!

Introduction

Microeconomics deals with the low-level economic issues. In this course, you will study a basic introduction to economics following with an introduction to microeconomics. You are going to learn what economic growth is and what its affects are.

Demand and Supply is explained in an easy to understand way. You can easily understand about the law of demand and supply. Demand and Supply, both are the basic principles of microeconomics.

Do you know about different low level markets that lie in microeconomics and their maximizers? If no, don't worry, after studying this course you can easily answer to microeconomic questions.

Productivity and Equity play important role in any society. You will study about these in detail. What are the public goods? Don't know? The answer is in the course. Competitive Markets for Goods and Services are incorporated so you can study about them and deal in a better way with your rivalries.

Without making the introduction longer, let us start studying the course.

CHAPTER 1: THE BASICS

Economics is a sociology that looks at how individuals pick among the options accessible to them. It is social on the grounds that it includes individuals and their conduct. It is a science in light of the fact that it utilizes, however much as could be expected, an exploratory methodology in its examination of decisions.

SCARCITY, CHOICE, AND COST

All decisions imply that one option is chosen over another. Selecting among options includes three thoughts vital to economics: scarcity, choice, and opportunity cost.

SCARCITY

Our assets are constrained. At any time, we have just so much land, such a variety of processing plants, so much oil, and such a large number of people. However, our needs, our wishes for the things that we can create with those assets, are boundless. We would constantly like more and better lodging, more and better training, more and better of basically everything.

On the off chance that our assets were additionally unlimited, we could say yes to each of our needs and there would be no economics. Since our assets are constrained, we can't say yes to everything. To say yes to one thing requires that we say no to another. Regardless, we must settle on decisions.

Our unlimited needs are ceaselessly colliding with the limit of our assets, constraining us to pick a few activities and to reject others. Scarcity is the state of choosing among choices. A scarce is one for which the decision of one option requires that another be surrendered.

Essentially everything is scarce. Consider the air we inhale, which is accessible in colossal quantity at no charge to us. Could air possibly be scarce?

The test of whether air is scarce is whether it has alternative uses. What uses would we be able to make the air? We inhale it. We pollute it when we drive our autos, warm our homes, or work our industrial facilities. As a result, a utilization of the air is as a garbage dump. We surely require the air to relax. Be that as it may, pretty much as unquestionably, we dump garbage in it. Those two uses are obviously different options for one another. The more garbage we dump in the atmosphere, the less healthy and desirable, it will be to relax. In the event that we choose we need to inhale clean air, we must cutoff the exercises that create contamination. Air is a scarce good in light of the fact that it has alternative uses.

Not all goods, on the other hand, go up against us with such decisions. A free good is one for which the decision of one use does not require that we surrender another. One sample of a free good is gravity. The way that gravity is holding you to the earth does not imply that your neighbor is compelled to float up into space! One individual's utilization of gravity is not a different option for someone else's utilization. There are relatively few free goods. Space, for instance, was a free good when the main use we made of it was to look at it. In any case, now, our utilization of space has come to the point where one use can be an alternative option for another. In this manner, even parts of space are scarce. Space will without a doubt turn out to be all the scarcer as we find better approaches to utilize it. Scarcity portrays for all intents and purposes everything. Thusly, the extent of economics is wide to be sure.

SCARCITY AND THE FUNDAMENTAL ECONOMIC QUESTIONS

The decisions we confront as a consequence of scarcity raise three arrangements of issues. Each economy must answer the accompanying inquiries:

What ought to be delivered?

Utilizing the economy's scarce assets to deliver one thing requires surrendering another. Delivering better instruction, for instance, may require reducing different services, for example, social insurance. A choice to safeguard a wild region requires surrendering different uses of the area. Each society must choose what it will create with its scarce assets.

In what manner ought to goods and services be created?

There are a wide range of decisions to be made in determining how goods and services ought to be created. Should a firm utilize a couple skilled or a great number of unskilled laborers? Should it produce in its own nation or would it be a good idea for it to utilize foreign plants? Should assembling firms utilize new or reused crude materials to make their products?

For whom ought to goods and services be delivered?

On the off chance that a good/service is created, a choice must be made about who will get it. For instance, delegates of the poorest countries on earth frequently whine that energy utilization per individual in the United States is 17 times more prominent than energy utilization per individual on the planet's 62 poorest nations. Pundits contend that the world's energy ought to be all the more equally designated. Should it? That is a "for whom" question.

Each economy must determine what ought to be created, how it ought to be delivered, and for whom it ought to be delivered. We should come back to these inquiries over and over.

Opportunity Cost

It is inside of the context of scarcity that financial analysts characterize what is maybe the most important idea in all of economics, the idea of opportunity cost. Opportunity cost is the estimation of the best option sworn off in settling on any decision.

The opportunity cost to you of reading the rest of this part will be the estimation of the best other use to which you could have put your time. In the event that you burn through $20 on a pruned plant, you have, all the while, surrendered the advantages of spending the $20 on pizzas or a soft cover book or a night at the motion pictures. On the off chance that the book is the most significant of those options, then the opportunity cost of the plant is the estimation of the pleasure you generally anticipated that would get from the book.

The idea of opportunity cost must not be mistaken for the price tag of a thing. Consider the cost of a school or college education. That incorporates the estimation of the best alternative utilization of cash spent for educational cost, charges, and books. Be that as it may, the most important cost of a school education is the value of forgone alternative uses of time spent studying and going to class as opposed to utilizing the time as a part of some other attempt. Student relinquishes that time with the expectations of significantly more income in future or in light of the fact that they put a worth on the chance to learn. Then again consider the cost of heading off to the specialist. Some portion of that cost is the value of the best alternative utilization of the cash required to see the specialist. However, the cost additionally incorporates the value of the best alternative utilization of the time required to see the specialist. The fundamental thing to find in the idea of opportunity cost is found for the sake of the idea. Opportunity cost is the value of the best opportunity renounced in a specific decision. It is not just the sum spent on that decision.

CHAPTER 2: MICROECONOMICS - AN INTRODUCTION

The field of economics is commonly isolated into two wide realms:

1. Microeconomics
2. Macroeconomics

Microeconomics is the branch of economics that spotlights on the decisions made by individual decision-making units in the economy, regularly consumers, and firms, and the effects those decisions have on individual markets. Macroeconomics is the branch of economics that spotlights on the effect of decisions on the aggregate, or total, level of economic movement. Why do tickets to the best shows cost to such an extent? How does the danger of an unnatural weather change influence real domain costs in beach front zones? Why do ladies wind up doing the majority of the housework? Why do senior subjects get rebates on public travel frameworks? These inquiries are for the most part viewed as microeconomic in light of the fact that they concentrate on individual units or markets in the economy.

Both microeconomics and macroeconomics offer consideration regarding individual markets. Be that as it may, in microeconomics that consideration is an end in itself; in macroeconomics it is gone for clarifying the development of major economic totals, the level of aggregate output, the level of livelihood, and the value level.

CHAPTER 3: ECONOMIC GROWTH

An increment in the physical quantity or in the nature of variables of production accessible to an economy or an innovative increase will permit the economy to deliver more goods and services; it will move the economy's production possibilities curve outward. The procedure through which an economy accomplishes an outward move in its production possibilities outcomes curve is called economic growth.

THE SOURCES OF ECONOMIC GROWTH

Economic growth suggests an outward move in an economy's production possibilities outcomes curve. Changing these will move the curve. Anything that expands the quantity or nature of the elements of production accessible to the economy or that enhances the innovation accessible to the economy adds to economic growth.

Consider, for instance, the emotional additions in human capital that have happened in the United States subsequent to the start of the previous century. In 1900, around 3.5% of U.S. laborers had finished secondary school education. By 2006, that rate climbed just about to 92. Less than 1% of the laborers in 1900 had moved on from school; as late as 1940 just 3.5% had moved on from school. By 2006, about 32% had moved on from school. Notwithstanding being better taught, today's laborers have gotten more and better skills at work. They bring significantly all the more economically valuable learning and abilities to their work than specialists did a century back.

In addition, the innovative changes that have happened inside of the previous 100 years have enormously lessened the time and exertion required to create most goods and services. Robotized production has gotten to be ordinary. Advancements in transportation (autos, trucks, and planes) have made the development of goods and individuals less expensive and speedier. A bewildering exhibit of new materials is accessible for assembling. What's more, the improvement of modern information technology, including PCs, programming, and interchanges hardware, that appeared to continue at amazing pace particularly amid the last years of the most recent century and proceeding to the present has changed the way we live and work.

GOVERNMENT IN A MARKET ECONOMY

The production possibilities model gives a menu of decisions among alternativecombinations of goods and services. Given those decisions, which combinations will be created?

In a market economy, this inquiry is replied in extensive part through the collaboration of individual purchasers and sellers. As we have as of now seen, the government assumes a part too. It may look to support more important utilization of a few goods and dishearten utilization of others. In the United States, for instance, duties forced on cigarettes demoralize smoking, while unique treatment of property assessments and home loan enthusiasm for the government salary expense empowers home proprietorship. The government may attempt to stop the production and utilization of a few goods inside and out, the same numbers of governments do with drugs, for example, heroin and cocaine. The government may supplement the private utilization of a few goods by creating a greater amount of them itself, the same number of U.S. urban communities do with greens and tennis courts. In different cases, there may be no private market for a good/service by any stretch of the imagination.

All countries likewise depend on the government to give resistance, authorize laws, and redistribute salary. Indeed, even market economies depend on the government to manage the exercises of private firms, to ensure the earth, to give training, and to create an extensive variety of different goods and services. Government's part may be constrained in a market economy; however it remains on a very basic level important.

CHAPTER 4: DEMAND AND SUPPLY

DEMAND

Every good/service has its own uncommon attributes that determine the quantity individuals are eager and ready to devour. One is the cost of the good/service itself. Other autonomous variables that are important determinants of demand incorporate purchaser inclinations, costs of related goods and services, salary, demographic qualities, for example, populace size, and purchaser desires. The quantity of pizzas individuals will buy, for instance, depend all that much on whether they like pizza. It likewise relies on upon the costs for options, for example, ground sirloin sandwiches or spaghetti. The quantity of specialist visits is prone to differ with pay; individuals with higher salaries are liable to see a specialist more frequently than individuals with lower wages. The demands for pizza, for specialist visits, and for lodging are unquestionably influenced by the age conveyance of the populace and its size.

While diverse variables assume distinctive parts in impacting the demands for distinctive goods and services, financial experts give careful consideration to one; the cost of the good/service. Given the values of the various variables that influence demand, a higher cost has a tendency to decrease the quantity people demand, and a lower cost tends to build it.

The law of demand is known as a law on the grounds that the consequences of innumerable studies are predictable with it. Without a doubt, you have watched one sign of the law. When all is said in done, we expect the law of demand to hold. Given the values of different variables that impact demand, a higher cost lessens the quantity demanded. A lower cost builds the quantity demanded. Demand curves, in short, incline descending.

Demographic Characteristics

The quantity of purchasers influences the aggregate quantity of a good/service that will be purchased; when all is said in done, the more important the populace, the more important the demand. Other demographic qualities can influence demand too. As the share of the populace over age 65 expands, the demand for restorative services, sea travels, and RVs increments. The conception rate in the United States fell pointedly somewhere around 1955 and 1975 yet has bit by bit expanded from that point forward. That increment has raised the demand for such things as baby supplies, grade teachers, soccer mentors, in-line skates, and school instruction. Demand can along these lines shift as an aftereffect of changes in both the number and attributes of purchasers.

Purchaser Expectations

The utilization of goods that can be effortlessly put away, or whose utilization can be delayed, is firmly influenced by purchaser desires. The desire of more up to date TV innovations, for example, top quality TV, could back off offers of general TVs. On the off chance that individuals anticipate that fuel costs will rise tomorrow, they will top off their tanks today to attempt to beat the cost increment. The same will be valid for goods, for example, autos and clothes washers: a desire of higher costs later on will prompt more purchases today. On the off chance that the cost of a good is relied upon to fall, in any case, individuals are liable to lessen their buys today and anticipate tomorrow's lower costs. The desire that PC costs will fall, for instance, can lessen current demand.

SUPPLY

What determines the quantity of a good/service sellers are willing to offer available to be purchased? Cost is one variable; ceteris paribus, a higher cost is prone to impel sellers to offer a greater quantity of a good/service. Production cost is another determinant of supply. Variables that influence production cost incorporates the costs of components used to deliver the good/service, comes back from option exercises, innovation, the desires of sellers, and normal occasions, for example, climate changes. Still another variable influencing the quantity of a good that will be offered available to be purchased is the quantity of sellers, the more important the quantity of sellers of a specific good or service, the more prominent will be the quantity offered at any value per time period.

Costs of Factors of Production

An adjustment in the cost of labor or some other component of production will change the cost of delivering any given quantity of the good/service. This adjustment in the cost of production will change the quantity that suppliers are willing to offer at any cost. An increment in product costs ought to diminish the quantity suppliers will offer at any value, moving the supply curve to one side. A decrease in component costs builds the quantity suppliers will offer at any value, moving the supply curve to one side.

CHAPTER 5: MARKETS, MAXIMIZERS, AND EFFICIENCY

To say that people expand is to say that they pick some target and after that they try to boost its quality. A sprinter might need to augment his or her speed; a lawmaker might need to maximize the likelihood that he or she will win the following decision. Business analysts give careful consideration to two gatherings of maximizers: consumers and firms. We expect that consumers look to boost utility and that organizations try to maximize economic profit, which is the distinction between aggregate income and aggregate cost. The costs included in this idea of economic profit are figured in the economic sense, as the opportunity costs, or estimation of the best opportunity sworn off.

The supposition of boosting conduct lies at the heart of economic examination. As we investigate its suggestions, on the other hand, we must remember the qualification in the middle of models and the real world. Our model expects that people settle on decisions in a way that accomplishes a most extreme quality for some clearly characterized objective. In utilizing such a model, financial analysts don't expect that individuals really experience the computations we will depict. What financial analysts do contend is that individuals' conduct is extensively predictable with such a model. Individuals may not deliberately look to boost anything, but rather they carry on as if they do.

THE ANALYSIS OF MAXIMIZING BEHAVIOR

The exercises of consumers and firms have advantages, and they likewise have opportunity costs. We expect that given these advantages and costs, consumers and firms will settle on decisions that maximize the net advantage of every movement, the aggregate advantage of the action short its chance cost.

On account of a company's decisions in production, for instance, the aggregate advantage of production is the income a firm gets from selling the product; the aggregate cost is the opportunity cost the firm acquires by delivering it. The net advantage is in this manner aggregate income less aggregate opportunity cost, or economic profit.

Market analysts keep up that with a specific end goal to boost net advantage, consumers and firms assess every movement at the edge, and they consider the extra advantage and the extra cost of another unit of the action. Should you "supersize" your request at McDonald's? Will the extra drink and the extra French Fries worth the additional cost? Should a firm contract one more specialist? Will the advantages to the firm of procuring this laborer be justified regardless of the extra cost of contracting him or her?

The negligible advantage is the sum by which an extra unit of an action expands its aggregate advantage. It is the sum by which the additional French Fries expand your fulfillment, or the additional income the firm hopes to get by employing another specialist. The peripheral cost is the sum by which an extra unit of an action builds its aggregate cost. You will pay more to supersize your McDonald's request; the company's labor costs will rise when it procures another specialist.

To determine the quantity of any action that will expand its net advantage, we apply the marginal decision rule: If the minor advantage of an extra unit of an action surpasses the negligible cost, the quantity of the movement ought to be expanded. On the off chance that the minimal advantage is not exactly the marginal cost, the quantity ought to be decreased. Net advantage is amplified at the time when marginal advantage squares with negligible cost. The marginal decision rule is at the heart of the economic state of mind. The guideline essentially says this: If the extra advantage of one more unit surpasses the additional cost, does it; if not, don't. This straightforward rationale gives us an intense instrument for the investigation of a decision. Maybe more than some other rule in the economic examination, the minor choice standard exemplifies the route in which financial experts dissect issues.

Maximizing decisions must be made inside of the parameters forced by some imperative, which is a limit that confines the scope of decisions that can be made. We accept that a customer looks for the greatest satisfaction possible inside of the points of confinement of his or her pay or spending plan. A firm can't create past the breaking points of its production limit at a point in time. The marginal decision rule shapes the establishment for the structure financial analysts use to examine all decisions. At first look, it may appear that a buyer looking for fulfillment from, say, pizza has little in a similar manner as a business person looking for profit from the production of specially crafted semiconductors. In any case, expanding decisions dependably take after the negligible choice principle, and that manage holds paying little respect to what is being augmented or who is doing the maximizing.

Boosting in the Marketplace

At the point when the net advantages of every single economic activity are boosted, market analysts say the allotment of assets is efficient. This idea of productivity is more extensive than the thought of efficient production that we experienced while examining the production possibilities outcomes curve. There, we saw that the economy's elements of production would be efficient in production in the event that they were allotted by the principle of near favorable position. That implied creating however much as could reasonably be expected with the variables of production accessible. The idea of an efficient designation of assets incorporates production, as in that dialog, however, it incorporates productivity in the utilization of goods and services too.

The Role of Property Rights

An easily working market requires that producers have property rights to the goods and services they create and that consumers have property rights to the goods and services they purchase. Property rights are an arrangement of standards that determine the routes in which a proprietor can utilize an asset. Consider the tomato market. Agriculturists who develop tomatoes have clearly characterized rights to their property and to the tomatoes they create and sell. Merchants who buy tomatoes from ranchers and sell them to food merchants have clear rights to the tomatoes until they sell them to food merchants. The food merchants who buy the tomatoes hold rights to them until they sell them to consumers. When you purchase a tomato, you have the restrictive right to its utilization.

An arrangement of property rights shapes the premise for all market exchange. Before the exchange can start, there must be a clear determination of who claims what. The arrangement of property rights should likewise demonstrate what buyers are obtaining when they purchase rights to specific assets. Since property rights must exist if the exchange is to happen, and in light of the fact that exchange is the procedure through which economic effectiveness is accomplished, an arrangement of property rights is vital to the efficient designation of assets.

Envision what might happen in the market for tomatoes if property rights were not plainly characterized. Assume, for instance, that merchants couldn't legitimately keep somebody from basically snatching some tomatoes and leaving without paying for them. On the off chance that that were the situation, merchants would not be liable to offer tomatoes available to be purchased. On the off chance that it was the situation for all basic need things, there would not be markets at all.

Despite the fact that property rights change for diverse assets, two qualities are required if the marketplace is to accomplish an efficient allotment of assets:

1. **Property rights must be exclusive**

A selective property right is one that permits its proprietor to keep others from utilizing the asset. The proprietor of a house, for instance, has the privilege to bar others from the utilization of the house. What's more, the failure to sell the property would constrain the motivation of proprietors to look after it.

2. **Property rights must be transferable.**

A transferable property right is one that permits the proprietor of an asset to sell or rent it to another person. Without transferability, no exchange could happen.

CHAPTER 6: PRODUCTIVITY AND EQUITY

Consumer demands are influenced by wages. Demand, all things considered, reflects capacity and also the eagerness to pay for goods and services. The market will be more receptive to the inclinations of individuals with high earnings than to those of individuals with low salaries.

In a market that fulfills the productivity condition, an efficient assignment of assets will rise up out of a specific appropriation of salary. Diverse salary conveyances will bring about distinctive, yet at the same time efficient, results. For instance, if 1% of the populace controls for all intents and purposes all the wage, then the market will efficiently dispense basically all its production to those same individuals.

What is a reasonable, or impartial, conveyance of pay? What is an uncalled for dissemination? Should everybody have the same pay? Is the present dispersion reasonable? Should the rich have less and the poor have more? Should the working class have more? Equity is all that much in the brain of the spectator. What may appear to be fair to one individual may appear to be biased to another. There is, notwithstanding, no test we can apply to determine whether the circulation of wage is or is not impartial. That question requires a standardizing judgment.

Determining whether the distribution of assets is or is not efficient is one issue. Determining whether the appropriation of salary is reasonable is another. The administrations of all countries act somehow to redistribute pay. That certainty proposes that individuals, for the most part, have inferred that leaving the circulation of pay singularly to the market would not be reasonable and that some redistribution is alluring. This may take the type of higher duties for individuals with higher earnings than for those with lower salaries. It may take the type of extraordinary projects, for example, welfare programs, for low-pay individuals.

Whatever circulation society picks, an efficient distribution of assets is still wanted to an inefficient one. Since an efficient designation expands net advantages, the increase in net advantages could be appropriated in a way that leaves all individuals preferable off over they would be at any inefficient distribution. In the event that an efficient allotment of assets appears to be uncalled for, it must be on the grounds that the conveyance of pay is out of line.

Market Failure

Private choices in the marketplace may not be predictable with the boost of the net advantage of a specific movement. The failure of private choices in the marketplace to accomplish an efficient distribution of scarce assets is called market failure. Markets won't produce an efficient distribution of assets on the off chance that they are not focused or if property rights are not very much characterized and completely transferable. Either condition will imply that leaders are not confronted with the minor advantages and costs of their decisions.

NONCOMPETITIVE MARKETS

The model of demand and supply accept that markets are focused. Nobody in these markets has any control over the harmony value; every buyer and maker takes the market cost as given and reacts to it. Under such conditions, a cost is determined by the convergence of demand and supply.

In a few markets, be that as it may, singular purchasers or sellers are sufficiently effective to impact the market cost.

CHAPTER 7: PUBLIC GOODS & PRODUCTION AND COST

A few goods are unrealistic to be delivered and exchanged in a market as a result of uncommon qualities of the goods themselves. The advantages of these goods are such that prohibition is not possible. Moreover, the peripheral cost of including one more purchaser is zero. A useful for which the cost of avoidance is restrictive and for which the minor cost of an extra client is zero is a public good.

National Defense is a public good. When resistance is given, it is unrealistic to bar individuals who have not paid for it from its utilization. Further, the cost of an extra client is zero, an armed force does not cost any more if there is one more individual to be secured. Different samples of public goods incorporate law authorization, fire insurance, and endeavors to protect species undermined with termination.

PUBLIC GOODS AND THE GOVERNMENT

Since numerous people who advantage from public goods won't pay for them, private firms will create a littler quantity of public goods than is efficient, in the event that they deliver them by any means. In such cases, it might be attractive for government offices to venture in. The government can supply a more prominent quantity of the great by direct procurement, by buying general society great from a private organization, or by financing utilization. Regardless, the cost is financed through tax collection and in this manner maintains a strategic distance from the free-rider issue.

Most public goods are given specifically by government offices. Governments produce national barrier and law implementation, for instance. Private firms under contract with government offices create some public goods. Park upkeep and flame services are public goods that are here and there created by private firms. In different cases, the administration advances the private utilization or production of public goods by financing them. Private altruistic commitments regularly bolster exercises that are public goods; elected and state governments sponsor these by permitting citizens to lessen their assessment installments by a small amount of the sum they contribute.

PRODUCTION AND COST

A wide range of production endeavors require decisions in the utilization of variables of production. In this part, we analyze such decisions. Should a good or service be created utilizing moderately more labor and less capital? Then again ought to generally more capital and less labor be utilized? Shouldn't something be said about the utilization of characteristic assets?

Financial experts expect that organizations take part in production so as to procure a profit and that they look to make this profit as extensive as could reasonably be expected. That is, financial analysts accept that organizations apply the negligible choice guideline as they try to boost their profits.

PRODUCTION CHOICES AND COSTS

Our analysis of production and cost starts with a period that financial experts call the *short run.* For instance, a restaurant may view its building as a fixed asset over a time of at least the following year. It would require in any event that much investment to locate another building or to extend or decrease the measure of its present office. Choices concerning the operation of the restaurant amid the following year must expect the building will stay unaltered. Different elements of production could be changed amid the year, yet the extent of the building must be viewed as a consistent.

The ideas of scarcity, decision, and opportunity cost are at the heart of economics. A good is scarce if the decision of one option requires that another be surrendered. The presence of options uses constrains us to settle on decisions.

While the supervisors of the restaurant are settling on decisions concerning its operation throughout the following year, they are additionally getting ready for longer periods. Over those periods, supervisors may consider options, for example, changing the building, building another office, or selling the building and leaving the restaurant business. The planning period over which a firm can consider all components of production as variable is known as the *long run.*

The supervisors may be planning what to accomplish for the following couple of weeks and for the following couple of years. Their choices throughout the following couple of weeks are prone to be *short-run decisions.* Choices that will influence operations throughout the following couple of years may be long-run decisions, in which supervisors can consider changing each part of their operations.

CHAPTER 8: COMPETITIVE MARKETS FOR GOODS AND SERVICES

For all intents and purposes, all organizations in a market economy face competition from different firms. Perfect competition is a model of the market in view of the suspicion that an extensive number of firms produce indistinguishable goods devoured by an expansive number of purchasers. The model of perfect competition additionally expects that it is simple for new firms to enter the market and for existing ones to take off. Lastly, it expects that purchasers and sellers have complete data about market conditions.

PRESUMPTIONS OF THE MODEL

The presumptions of the model of perfect rivalry, taken together, infer that individual purchasers and sellers in a superbly focused market acknowledge the market cost as given. Nobody, purchaser or seller, has any impact over that cost. People or firms who must take the market cost as given are called price takers. A buyer or firm that takes the market cost as given has no capacity to impact that cost. A price-taking firm or customer is similar to a person who is purchasing or selling stocks. He or she gazes upward the market price and purchases or sells at that cost. The cost is determined by demand and supply in the market, not by individual purchasers or sellers. In a consummately focused market, every firm and every purchaser is a price taker. A price-taking buyer accepts that he or she can buy any quantity at the market cost, without influencing that cost. Likewise, a price-taking firm accepts it can sell whatever quantity it wishes at the market cost without influencing the cost.

You are a price taker when you go into a store. You watch the costs recorded and settle on a decision to purchase or not. Your decision won't influence that cost.

PERFECT COMPETITION AND THE REAL WORLD

The presumptions of indistinguishable products, a huge number of buyers, easy entry and exit, and perfect information are solid presumptions. The thought that organizations must sit back and let the market determine price appears to contradict what we think about most real firms, which is that organizations usually do set costs. Yet this is the premise for the model of demand and supply, the force of which you have as of now seen.

When we utilize the model of demand and supply, we accept that market strengths determine costs. In this model, purchasers and sellers react to the market cost. They are price takers. The presumptions of the model of perfect competition underlie the presumption of price taking conduct.

In this manner, we are utilizing the model of perfect competition at whatever point we apply the model of demand and supply.

We can see most markets by applying the model of demand and supply. Despite the fact that those markets don't satisfy every one of the suppositions of the model of perfect completion, the model permits us to see some key components of these markets.

CONCLUSION

Hope so this course has been a worth for you. Do you like reading the course? Was it helpful? Are there any suggestions? Don't forget to review about it.

Thanks a lot for reading, and I wish you very best of luck for your future life.

Goodbye!

ABOUT THE AUTHOR

Can Akdeniz is entrepreneur, consultant and book author. He is regarded as one of the most inspiring business authors of our time.

His books address an array of important business topics from general topics like productivity to more specific topics like the value of being seen as a "cool boss." In addition to running the acclaimed business blog businesshacker.co .

Can has released numerous books that have collectively changed the way people think about business and achieving success.

Check More Books by Can Akdeniz
http://www.amazon.com/Can-Akdeniz/e/B00DJPQA34/

Can's Blog
http://businesshacker.co

Follow on Twitter
https://twitter.com/canakdeniz1981

36010312R00028

Made in the USA
Middletown, DE
21 October 2016